Praise for *The DNA of Leadership:*

"General Dick Abel is a great man of prayer and a teacher of God's Word. He is a spirit-filled leader who has led the Fellowship of Christian Athletes and directed the ministry of Campus Crusade for Christ to the Military. He has risen to the top in serving in the U.S. Air Force. His love and compassion follow him in every area of life. This book demonstrates his principles of leadership."

Anne Graham Lotz

"*The DNA of Leadership* is an excellent reflection of a lifetime of 'lessons learned' from a true leader. Dick Abel is a role model for his insight that 'leadership is all about people.' Dick has been a consistent example of servant leadership in multiple roles over many years."

Tim Tassopoulos
Senior Vice President, Operations
Chick-Fil-A

"In *The DNA of Leadership* Dick Abel has given us a concise but meaningful discussion of the attributes, challenges and rewards of being a principled and effective leader. He has led the life, knows the subject matter, and given anyone who would hope to productively lead in any walk of life a great reference work."

Ron Fogleman
General, USAF (Ret)
Chief of Staff, Air Force, 1994–1997

"There is a critical need for strong leadership in our country. General Dick Abel presents the essentials in this book, which I highly recommend to all who seek success as leaders in their home and business."

Roger Staubach
Executive Chairman
The Staubach Company
Former Dallas Cowboy

"I got to know Dick Abel when he was the President of the Fellowship of Christian Athletes. Dick brings a great deal of experience and credibility to the table as he discusses leadership. His military background and his years of running the Fellowship of Christian Athletes enable him to observe very clearly what works and what doesn't work in leading others."

Tom Osborne
Former Head Football Coach
University of Nebraska

"Dick Abel is a true American hero and inspiring leader. The principles in *The DNA of Leadership* provide a framework for developing your own leadership talents. His message will engage and motivate leaders."

Ike Skelton
US Congressman
Chairman of the House Armed Services Committee

"Dick Abel has dedicated his entire life to improving leadership. You'll find his approach to leadership to be both instructing and inspiring. Enjoy!"

Vern Clark
Admiral, US Navy (Ret)

THE DNA OF
LEADERSHIP

THE DNA OF
LEADERSHIP
Leadership is All About People

BY BRIG. GENERAL DICK ABEL
FOREWORD BY GENERAL RICHARD B. MYERS, US AIR FORCE RET.
FORMER CHAIRMAN, JOINT CHIEFS OF STAFF

18 Characteristics that Develop Great Leaders at Work & Home

TATE PUBLISHING & *Enterprises*

Published by Tate Publishing & Enterprises, LLC
127 E. Trade Center Terrace | Mustang, Oklahoma 73064 USA
1.888.361.9473 | www.tatepublishing.com

Tate Publishing is committed to excellence in the publishing industry. The company reflects the philosophy established by the founders, based on Psalm 68:11,
"The Lord gave the word and great was the company of those who published it."

Published in the United States of America

ISBN: 978-1-60604-576-3
1.Business & Economics / Leadership

08.12.03

DEDICATION

This book is dedicated to Ann, my beloved wife of more than fifty years, and our four children and nineteen grandchildren. Collectively, they have set the bar of what character should be in my life.

This is also dedicated to the men and women of the Armed Forces, from the youngest recruit in basic training to the most senior leader, including the Chairman of the Joint Chiefs of Staff. At all levels in my thirty years of active duty in the United States Air Force and fourteen years as Executive Director of the Military Ministry of Campus Crusade, I have learned immeasurably from the character, commitment, loyalty, and work ethic of these dedicated men and women who are our peace keepers. They are my heroes.

ACKNOWLEDGEMENT

To Karen Trimble, my special assistant at the Military Ministry and a helper in producing this book.

To my mighty men, George Toles, Tim Tassopolous, Tony Batezel, Dan Arnold, and Don Hilkemeier. They have provided editorial assistance and personal encouragement to me. Each man is a successful leader in his life and an example to me.

To the commanders, coaches, chaplains, and community leaders who have had a profound influence on my life.

To the Godly champions who are prayer warriors that helped me to know God and His great love for me in Jesus so I can have eternal life.

TABLE OF CONTENTS

Foreword	13
Introduction	15
Principles of Successful Leaders	19
Integrity	23
Knowledge	29
Decisiveness	33
Courage	37
Dependability	41
Discipline	45
Delegation	49
Vision	53
Justice	57
Example	61
Communication	67
Sensitivity	71
Human Responsibility	75
Confidence	79
Teamwork	83
Training	87
Relaxation	91
Love	97
Conclusion	101
Leadership Quiz	103
Appendix	107
About the Author	109
Additional Endorsements	111

FOREWORD

The leadership environment today is as challenging and demanding as it's ever been. The margin for error is narrow and the world unforgiving of poor performance. Whether it's national security concerns, economic worries, or the environment, we have many difficult issues and decisions ahead. Some of the most critical issues won't wait as time, in many cases, isn't on our side. In the beginning of the 21st Century we need one thing for sure if we are to succeed—and that's strong leadership. And strong leadership means leaders with great character.

Great character can be defined in many ways. I think most people agree that it means leaders with great integrity. Men and women who do what they say they'll do and have the courage to always do what they think is right. It also means we need leaders who are serving selflessly, serving something bigger than themselves. In addition, our rapidly changing environment means our leaders must be able to think agilely and flexibly about new issues.

Dick Abel does a beautiful job of talking about "strong" leadership—leadership that emphasizes character as the basis of motivating people to get things done. He also does a wonderful job talking about eighteen principles of successful leaders and makes these principles come alive so you can learn and measure yourself against them. There isn't such a thing as a cookbook on how to be a good leader, but *The DNA of Leadership* comes as close as anything I've read.

If you are leading people today or have the aspiration to lead people in the future, this book is a must for you. It does not matter what your previous leadership experience has been, the fact is you will gain insight and confidence from reading *The DNA of Leadership*. If current and future leaders embrace the concepts outlined in Dick Abel's work, we'll be empowering and treating people in a way that will make all of us more productive and happy. And in the end the world will be a better place.

Richard B. Myers
General, US Air Force, Ret.
Former Chairman, Joint Chiefs of Staff

INTRODUCTION

God created each of us to be "somebody." We are each unique in our personalities, finger prints and DNA. There is none other like us. The question then is "Who are we—really?"

Regardless of where we work or live the question remains the same—who are we? People are the key to success or failure in every home, business, team, school, and venue in this world. That is why leadership is all about people.

The DNA of Leadership may seem an obvious title for this book, as each of us is unique with a variety of leadership characteristics. People in business, on athletic teams, in the military, and pastors, endorsed the idea if it weren't for people, leadership would be much easier. The DNA of the people they are leading is also diverse. I've found the same experience myself.

Today, more than at any time in history, there is a need for leaders of strong character. My friend Chuck Swindoll stated it well: "Know who you are, like who you are, and be who you are."

Some of us have been mentored by wonderful people, but we should not attempt to become our mentor's mirror image. We have to be our own person. We must understand who we are, then embrace characteristics in our lives that will affect who we are and how we can impact other people. Chuck Swindoll, in his book Leadership, defines this as "inspired influence."

If we are to be people who inspire others to greatness, we must be of sound character. WorldCom, Enron, and many other now defunct companies are examples of how the leadership failed—when the senior executives started to think too highly of themselves. Leaders gave up on the basic fundamentals they had learned, then were side-tracked by the pressures of the job, demands of society, or stresses at home. They forgot that success is…"all about people."

In these pages we will review some bedrock principles of character.

They are the foundation we need to build upon. Character is who we are 24/7. It's who we are at home, on the job … and when no one is looking. Character is not inherited, but developed in our daily life.

Character forms our lasting reputation and will be our legacy. Building a moral and ethical lifestyle should be our main goal in life. In their in-flight magazine, the President of Southwest Airline says, "SWA culture permeates every aspect of our culture. It is our essence, our DNA, our past, our present and our future."

"It's not just knowing the right thing to do, it's having the courage to do it," said General John Jumper, United States Air Force.

"Your image, who you want people to believe you are; your reputation is what they believe and say about you; your character is who you really are," according to Vice Admiral Scott Redd, U.S. Navy, retired, another mentor of mine.

In other words, our character is the DNA of each of us.

Abraham Lincoln advised us, "Nearly all men can stand adversity, but if you want to test a man's character, give him power."

Give people power; give them leadership roles and see how they perform—that's when their character is really tested.

Character is not made in crisis; it is manifested in stressful times. Character is more important than competence. It is not something we put on when we leave the house, like a business suit or uniform. Character is habitual. It's what runs through our veins. It's standing for what's right even when our position is unpopular. Leadership is the outward expression of our inner character.

Coach Bill McCartney nails it by saying, "The measure of a man's character can be found in the face of his wife."

John Maxwell, an author, speaker, and respected authority on leadership, says, "If you wouldn't follow yourself, why should anyone else follow you?"

Your image is who you want people to think you are; your reputation is who people think you are; your character is who you really are. Character is not a matter of outward techniques, but of inward reality. Character is made up of all you stand for. Some people will compromise their character if they think it will get them ahead.

As you read and think through *The DNA of Leadership*, consider using this book as a study guide or checklist for your own life. It should not be something that is read, noted, and then put on the shelf to gather dust. This book is designed to be reviewed periodically to keep one "on the mark," to hold you accountable. Yes, accountability groups are good, but there is also the need for us to provide accountability and discipline in our own lives, and *The DNA of Leadership* will help to serve that purpose.

As we review these eighteen characteristics, each one will be balanced and discussed for application in your venue. We will speak of the impact they can have and talk about hurdles we face. As a former coach, it's my prayerful desire that the following pages will equip and propel you to be the "all star" leader in your home, community, church, and your marketplace.

View the characteristics as essential in the home. If you are married you may conclude that we're presenting guidance or marriage counseling. Remember the need to be that 24/7 honest, moral, ethical person in and out of your family environment.

PRINCIPLES OF
SUCCESSFUL LEADERS

During the last quarter of the 20th century there was a tremendous focus on management. At whatever price you could afford, you could attend a "life-changing" seminar, buy a book, or download material on the "scientific art" of management. Manage, manage, manage. As technology ramped up and communication expanded at an exponential rate, we focused more and more on management.

Then in the 1990's, the trend began to shift to a realization that we lead people and manage resources. There is a very clear distinction between the two.

A computer or any machinery has no emotions, feelings, heart, or spirit. People have these qualities. That's why people are so mission-critical. We manage resources and lead people.

When we try to manage people, we ultimately fail. You've seen it happen. When you come upon a leader interested in his people, that's when positive changes occur. Managers must also be leaders if they are to be successful and need to realize the difference between managing and leading.

In this chapter we will discuss very basic, proven principles that are the foundation for all of the characteristics. These maxims are important because they're the building blocks of our character if we're going to be authentic and successful leaders.

"To Be's" of leadership:

- *"To Be" a Servant-Leader.* Effective leaders will serve those who are following them. Your greatness is not how many serve you, but how many people you serve, and how well you serve them. General Robert E. Lee was asked by a soldier, "How can I raise my son?" Lee thought for a moment, and then responded, "Teach your son to deny himself." By human nature, we don't like to deny ourselves. Putting others first, and being servant-leaders is the surest sign of a genuine leader. Serving others will be seen in our actions and words and reflect quiet strength.

- *"To Be" a Leader of Compassion.* People don't really care how much you know until they know how much you care. When commanders change in the military, the usual process is for the gaining unit to get a photo and a biographical sketch of the new "top gun." Most people in the unit want to know who their new boss is, what she or he looks like, and all about his or her background and experience. The corporate world does the same when senior leadership changes.

Then the question comes "Who is this person, really? Do they have a compassionate spirit? Do they care about things other than themselves? Will they care about you?" Good leaders seek to get close enough to feel the heartbeat of their people, which allows positive influence for their employee in good times and bad. Compassion is foundational to being a successful leader.

- *"To Be" People of Conviction.* When President Gerald Ford was laid to rest, people praised him as a man of conviction, even though he took many "hits" because of some of his decisions. He had standards of what was right, and he did the right thing. Our challenge is to know the right thing, do the right thing, and do it for the right reason. Strong leaders are not moved by the polls, the press, or by other pressures that would sway them to violate their own boundaries. General Ron Fogelman, former Chief of Staff of the U.S. Air Force, retired early "on principle." He would not violate his absolute belief concerning one of his fellow flag officers who was being targeted as a scapegoat for the Kobar Towers terrorist attack in Saudi Arabia.

We suffer from the pursuit of comfort rather than conviction… of accommodation rather than truth… of a pleasant life rather than a meaningful life. To lead and serve, one must be trustworthy and committed to the truth. As Max Lucado says: "Some leaders seek the applause of men when in fact we should seek the applause of heaven."

> Wes Anderson has said, "Conviction is not measured in the happiness of the leader, but doing the right thing, the right way, for the right reason."

Each of us has a choice to make: we are either going to be a person of conviction or a chameleon. The choice is ours. Are we locked in tight to what we believe is Truth, or do we conform to the flow of society with people wondering what we stand for? One who is merely politically correct "is like a leaf in the wind". No one knows where it will settle. Your impact as a person of strong character will have a positive effect on all who you lead. The question is, are you a person of conviction or a chameleon? The choice is yours.

- *"To Be" Consistent.* Serving others and doing the right thing for your people with consistency is how we should lead and live our daily lives. Not only in our beliefs, but in our manners, our respect, and our loyalty. As we live consistent lives others will rely on us.

These principles are foundational to mentoring people so they can grow and mature and learn to have the strength of character others can follow and practice.

The following chapters specifically focus on traits that apply in the home as well as the marketplace. Each stands alone; however, when integrated they reflect who you "really are." You can be a strong leader. Strong leaders are not just born; they develop. *The DNA of Leadership* will help you and your team become All-Stars.

INTEGRITY

Swear to tell the truth and nothing but ...

Trustworthy

Integrity is at the top of the list in every leadership session I've attended in the last fifty years. Why is it so significant to your employees? Your spouse? Or your children? The answer: because it builds security, trust, confidence, and credibility. Your commitment to being a person of integrity defines your total character.

What is integrity? It is: "absolute wholeness, truthfulness, unblemished, undivided, without imperfection, sound moral principles, and trustworthiness." The Bible says, "He who walks in integrity walks securely." This priceless quality is the hallmark of a great leader.

> Ralph Waldo Emerson once poignantly said, "What you do speaks so loudly I can't hear what you are saying."

President Gerald Ford was a synonym for integrity. His word was always good. He had high values, was a humble man of principle, and never compromised his convictions. Here's a man you'd want to be involved with in business or have as a friend.

Integrity is "who you are in the dark, when no one is looking." That's true all of the time, 24/7. Integrity is not a ninety percent thing. You either have it or you don't. It is a very important part of your DNA.

President Reagan said that character is a habit we don't have to think about it. You don't get up in the morning, leave the house, and say, "Today I'm going to be a person of integrity." It's habitual. It's in your veins. It's inescapable—like your shadow or your fingerprints or your DNA. It's who you really are.

The 40th President of the United States said:

> The character that takes command in moments of crucial choices has already been determined by a thousand other choices made earlier in seemingly unimportant moments. It has been determined by all the 'little' choices of years past—by all those times when the voice of conscience was at war with the voice of temptation ... whispering the lie that 'it really doesn't matter.' It has

been determined by all the day-to-day decisions made when life seemed easy and crises seemed far away—the decisions that, piece by piece, bit by bit, developed habits of discipline or laziness; habits of self-sacrifice or self-indulgence; habits of duty and honor and integrity—or dishonor and shame.

Ronald Reagan

Mark Twain said, "Always tell the truth; that way you don't have to have a good memory."

People want a leader they can trust. In marriage, trust is a minimum daily requirement. No trust, no future.

An old Chinese proverb says, "To starve to death is a small thing, but to lose one's integrity is a great one."

An Air Force general insists that integrity is not elastic. One only has to visit a ball bearing plant to understand why the integrity of one of those spheres is so important. A ball bearing is made to absolute specifications so that when it is put in place, the machine will work. However, if beneath its perfect exterior there's a blemish inside, when the bearing is heated and pressure comes, the ball bearing can explode. The result would be catastrophic. Your life may be like that. If integrity is not rock solid throughout all you do, then when you face challenges, when you're under severe stress, you'll lose your bearing, and your integrity can implode.

The impact of integrity in our home or organization is what builds trust, faith, credibility, and confidence, and will help create sound teamwork. You cannot get by without strong, habitual integrity. A building is only as strong as its foundation and our lives are only as good as the foundation of our character. Take a cornerstone away from a building and it will fall. Take the cornerstone of integrity away from your life and your world will be leveled. When this happens, and trust is broken, only the violater can restore faith. When trust is shattered with a mate, an employee, a peer, or a boss, it can only be restored when the one "violated" is given reason to trust again.

A business acquaintance working in the securities field was surprised when a friend and client lied about an investment. After attempts to clear up the disagreement failed, the client brought a major lawsuit against his friend. Efforts were made to correct the relationship, but due to continuing lack of credibility, trust could not be restored.

Sadly, our society has devalued integrity. Schools of higher learning that have honor codes demand integrity and honesty. Young people from across the entire spectrum of our country's culture are represented at these institutions. Some come from homes where parents, grandparents, teachers, coaches, ministers, and others have instilled in them the disciplines of integrity and courage. They've been taught to be a person of integrity. Unfortunately, many of the institutions of higher learning are moving students away from their former convictions. The superintendant at of one of our service academies has said that a percentage of new cadets believe that lying isn't wrong unless you get caught.

These young people may be from homes where this thing called "integrity" is AWOL. Without standards or accountability, these kids lapsed into thinking, "I did it my way and that's okay." My way may not be the right way. Perhaps this may be why our country and even the world faces staggering problems including:

- Loosening of Wholesome Controls.

- Lowering of Moral Standards.

- Lack of Parental Restraint in.

- Loss of Divine Power.

Integrity comes from the word "integer," a math term for a whole number that cannot be divided. It's intact, entire, and complete. Billy Graham has said that we must consistently strive to keep our integrity intact. Without integrity, we are non-starters.

Roger Staubach, a Heisman Trophy winner from the Naval Academy and an All-Pro quarterback for the Dallas Cowboys, said in Success magazine, "Be honest … it's all about integrity, values and trust."

It's up to you to be the "I" in Integrity …

KNOWLEDGE

Mind Over Matter

Getting the facts down

Knowledge is defined as the acquisition of facts, truth, particular principles, systems, units, and commands. It is all of the aspects of business and communication. Knowledge is also the wisdom of knowing how to be a good spouse, parent, grandparent, and leader.

Today there is more information available than we can absorb. In past generations, when trying to gain knowledge, people visited the library or turned to a set of encyclopedias at home and delved into them to dig for information. Now there is more knowledge available at our finger tips through electronic technology than ever before.

Knowledge is available through other people. Some acquire knowledge from their leaders, teachers, peers, parents, grandparents, mentors, and through experience as well as information gained from media, both print and visual. We begin acquiring basic knowledge at an early age. Unfortunately, many youngsters are now being raised from birth outside the home, thus lacking parental influence and guidance.

Today, with the electronic access to volumes and volumes of material, we can receive information on any subject, and in great detail. If you're an accountant you can learn all of the new methods of being the best accountant for your organization via the internet. In human resources the same is true. There is no limit of information on any subject or venue. The well-read person also knows current events and is capable of interacting within a multitude of environments and diverse people groups.

The most successful leaders are those who know their own role and responsibilities, and how they fit into every aspect of the organization, command, business, etc. They become experts. Knowledge comes from having a view of the complete picture and not just one's own area of involvement. The broader your knowledge of the total operation, the more effective and valuable you will be, inside and outside your organization.

Broad knowledge allows us to be a player in any forum. "Choose knowledge rather than gold," a proverb says, and we know the value of gold. Another advises, "Wise men store up knowledge; wisdom comes from God." The fear of God is the beginning of wisdom.

Professional knowledge will bring confidence and encouragement to the people you're leading. Without it, you're merely a clanging cymbal or a hollow gong, speaking empty words.

Hurdles in our quest for more knowledge are laziness, procrastination, lack of personal discipline, and misplaced priorities that deflect our attention from the work at hand.

How do the people you admire amass so much knowledge? Tap into their wealth of wisdom and you'll accelerate your search for contextual and actionable information.

President Abraham Lincoln said, "I will study and prepare myself and someday my chance will come."

If you are really seeking wisdom, surround yourself with people more knowledgeable than yourself. Learn how to motivate them to accomplish the job, mission, or task before you.

All leaders should be ready to learn from the circumstances the Lord puts them through; both positive and negative experience can be instructional.

DECISIVENESS

To the Right or to the Left?

Determined

Yogi Berra, the great New York Yankee player and manager, said, "When you come to the 'Y' in the road, take it."

That is exactly what some in leadership roles do ... they fail to or don't have the courage to make decisions. Yet that is what leaders, by virtue of their position, are expected to do. Avoiding making a decision is a decision in itself.

As I repeatedly ask groups of mid-level leaders if they ever worked for someone who couldn't or wouldn't make a decision, almost one hundred percent of them say "Yes." Leaders lead and are responsible for making decisions, "to the right or to the left." They're in the position to provide inspired influence, to motivate, communicate, and be involved in the lives of their people. They're also required to make decisions.

Decision, by definition, is picking a course of action. Wise leaders use talented people for input before making a critical decision. Some decisions may be unpopular, but if you have integrity and confidence and the trust of the people you lead then the choices you make will be more readily accepted.

Major General Perry Smith USAF (Ret) estimates that "prudent decisions are normally made when the leader has about sixty percent of the information."

You do not need all of the information before making a decision. Experience has shown that when you expect to have one hundred percent of the input you want, you will, in probability, not make a decision.

The ability to make tough calls is a unique gift. Training, knowledge, integrity, courage and input from your leadership team can result in making prompt decisions. Announced decisions in a clear, positive way brings the team together. Leaders must communicate with their team. Input from your senior leadership team (i.e. those around you) is essential. It certainly is preferred to being dictatorial.

The Manthei Company's leadership team meets weekly to review business operations. To stay on track they routinely discuss leadership examples. Decisions that come from these meetings are then announced to the company.

There are times when, because of unusual circumstances, your knowledge may cause you to make a decision independently, without input from your team. When this occurs, tell your team you're making the decision based on information that you cannot share with them at this time and that you stand by your decision. My experience has shown that when I made those independent decisions, which was very seldom, and I told the team why I was convinced it was the proper decision, I was correct in about eighty-five percent of the cases. What happened in the other fifteen percent? I had to go to the leadership team and say that I had made a mistake and suggest we go back to the drawing board to come up with another option. There is nothing wrong with saying "I made a mistake." There is nothing wrong with saying "Let's study it again; I need your input."

When you ask for advice from your colleagues, it builds their self-esteem and sense of teamwork. It assures them you have confidence in them and ultimately they will be more useful in fulfilling their responsibilities.

COURAGE

Gird Up Your Loins

Proceeding without fear

A former POW in Viet Nam wrote, "Courage is not the absence of fear, but the presence of faith."

In my observation, courage is the most lacking characteristic of leadership today. Political correctness seems to guide many people, leaders included.

Courage is the ability to stand up and proceed without fear on a course of action recognizing that you might be criticized or put into a dangerous position because of the stand you're about to take. Without courage you cannot be a person of integrity. Courage is being strong and courageous, not discouraged or fearful of failure.

Our greatest glory is not in never failing, but it is rising up every time we fail [see Proverbs 24:16].

You've heard it before: "If you get thrown off a horse, get back on." Don't be afraid to try and try again. Abraham Lincoln won the Presidency on his thirteenth attempt to be elected to public service.

Joe Thiesmann, the All-Pro quarterback for the Washington Redskins, had his knee completely torn apart in an NFL game. You may have seen the replay of that incident, and the courage shown as he left the field. Another example of strong courage is reflected by the great Americans who have lost limbs serving our country, yet want to return to their units as soon possible. That's courage and commitment.

President Ronald Reagan said, "There are no easy answers, but there are simple answers. We must have the courage to do what is morally right." In order to accomplish this, there must be moral standards.

Do you have the courage to do the right thing, the right way, for the right reason?

As we apply courage to our lives, it will transcend the characteristics and principles in this book. Courage is essential for success. We need to apply it just as we exhibit all the characteristics of our "person." You can't be decisive without being courageous. When you display courage, people can truly rely on you.

Being politically correct is doing what others think we ought to do in order to get ahead, instead of doing or saying what we know to be the right thing. A recent example of courage is found in the book Black Hawk Down. Squad leader, now U.S. Army chaplain, Jeff Struecker displayed courage at the highest level.

While in Somalia, he was exiting the battle zone when his gunner was shot in the head and killed. When SGT Struecker returned to base camp he was ordered to return to the battle area to rescue Americans still there. After ordered to do so, SGT Struecker cleaned up his bloody Humvee and drove back into harm's way. That required great courage.

At Parris Island Marine Recruit Training Center the recruits go through a number of obstacles in the "Crucible" training. Before each event, their squad leaders show them a picture of a Medal of Honor (MOH) recipient and read the accompanying citation. Most MOH's are presented posthumously. The recruits are given a vivid example of the courage of those who have gone before, thus setting a high bar for them as they get their "globe and anchor" and become Marines.

Courage is one characteristic you need to apply and make part of your life. People gain respect for courageous leaders who have a strong level of conviction and not politically correct. It is best summed up in the inscription on the Iwo Jima Memorial in Washington, D.C., "Uncommon valor was a common virtue."

DEPENDABILITY

Lean on Me

Ability to be counted on

Today, more than ever, the people who work with and for us want to depend on their leader. In many cases, our society has children and adults who find no "anchor" in their lives—no one to lean on. The definition of dependability is: a certainty of performance; a reliability; the ability to be counted on; someone who will never leave you or forsake you; someone who has your best interest in mind, someone you can go to at any moment. Dependability is working in a way that people can come to you, not only with things pertaining to their particular job, but also with personal challenges. They can approach you about problems in their marriage, with their children, finances, home, parents, or any other issue. Dependability means you are someone your people can count on.

> Coach Bill McCartney, former coach of the University of Colorado and founder of Promise Keepers, said this about the whole issue of coaching, "I believe in you—and when you believe in someone they can come to you."

Not that you are a crutch as some may think. As a leader, you know those on your team who may need a shoulder or back to lean on. Being available builds confidence and peace in those who see the world as a frightening place. Composer Bill Withers writes, "Lean on me when you're not strong, and I'll be your friend, I'll help you carry on."

A true and authentic leader will never leave you or forsake you. Are you someone people can trust and lean on? This is an important application to put into practice as you work with people. Remember the subtitle of this book, "Leadership Is All About People." One of your responsibilities in leadership is to always be involved with and available to those you lead, and always be there for them.

If your mate, employees, children, and others are not depending on you, be alert; you never know who is providing the influence in their lives.

The impact of the organization is quite obvious. The characteristic of dependability helps draw the team together to build and mature them into one with confidence, determination, and a high work ethic. When people can depend on you, it may drain your strength at the moment, but will invigorate you later.

That happened to me late one night when we were stationed in Hawaii at Pacific Command. About midnight one night, a Navy captain called and asked if we could visit. I suggest a time the next morning. He said, "No, I need to see you right now." So I had him come to our house and he told me of his problems in his family, with his children, and the hollowness he felt in his life. After two hours of sharing some thoughts and God's love, he made a decision to accept the Lord Jesus as his Savior. The next morning I was invigorated recalling that late night visit. The captain and I had a relationship which gave him confidence that he could call on and rely upon me.

Some hurdles to overcome when it comes to dependability are our own self-centeredness, our own pride. Pride can impact the whole issue of the characteristic of dependability. Nancy DeMoss spoke in 1995 to a gathering of leaders on the issue of pride. Here are five of the thirty points she presented comparing prideful and humble leaders. As you read these points, they may resonate with you as to your own life and help keep your focus off yourself and on others.

Proud, Unbroken People	Broken People
Focus on the failure of others	Are overwhelmed with their own spiritual need
Are self righteous; have critical fault-finding spirit	Are compassionate; have a forgiving spirit; look for the best in others
Look down on others	Esteem all others better than self
Are independent; have self-sufficient spirit	Have dependent spirit; recognize others' needs
Maintain control; must have their own way	Surrender control

DISCIPLINE

Your Borders in Life

Behavior maintained by training and control

Discipline is the positive molding of our lives that produces good character. It should not be confused with punishment, the correcting of others. When using this word in the leadership context, we mean personal discipline. It is the checks or restraints we place on our own actions and reactions. It is, as they say out West, "bringing in the fence lines."

Discipline is training to act in accordance with the acceptable rules of conduct. It is behavior that results in self-control, and acting in accordance with rules and regulations.

We live in a culture where discipline may seem like a forgotten characteristic. "Just do it" is one of the most popular logos on the market today. Problems result when we take it from the market place and apply it in a negative way in our lives. It then becomes the guide for our selfish and uncontrolled behavior.

> Coach John Wooden, the famous UCLA basketball coach and mentor of many, said, "Discipline yourself so someone else does not have to."

Practice self-control. Be a person of orderly conduct. Train yourself to know the rules and then live by them.

Lt. General John Jackson is president of Fork Union Military Academy in Virginia. A young man we knew was a student there, and was fully qualified and possessed potential for future success. We went to visit him and met in the president's office prior to going to lunch. When the young lad arrived, General Jackson offered these words of encouragement to him. "It is easy to succeed here; you just have to know the rules and obey them." This is one of the basics of success. If we will practice self-discipline, we are on our way to becoming successful, in our home, business, school, etc.

Doing the right thing, the right way, for the right reason, is another one of the keys of success. Living a disciplined life takes courage. It is helpful to have one or two responsible friends to hold us accountable.... friends that will ask us the tough questions in our journey of self-discipline. For the most part, friends interact super-ficially—"How's the weather, your health, been on any trips lately?" How would you answer if someone asked, "What are the main temp-tations you are wrestling with?" Or perhaps, "How is your relation-ship with your mate?" Or, "What legacy do you want to leave behind when you leave this world?"

A friend of ours was known to respond to questions or complaints: "Do you want me to tell you what you want to hear, or what you need to hear?" We profit from having people in our lives who will lovingly tell us what we need to hear. Know this: a disciplined life results in a life of significance, one that will continue to encourage folks long after we are gone.

The 2008 Olympics opening ceremony was an extraordinary example of discipline and training. If you saw the 100 plus drummers playing in unison you observed discipline on display.

So, do the right thing, the right way, for the right reason. Just do it!

DELEGATION

Over to You

To give authority to another

So you think you can do it all. You believe you don't need anyone even though you have people around you who have capabilities that you do not necessarily possess, which is probably the reason you hired them in the first place. Delegation is one of the key techniques of being a good leader. Delegation is allowing talented team members to use their gifts and expertise to accomplish their assigned tasks. In today's vernacular, one can say it is to empower your people—empower them to take on a task that will challenge them and increase their self-esteem and confidence. Delegation builds teamwork.

Delegate or die. To delegate is to share the workload, to entrust others with the authority and hold them responsible for completing the task. If you don't delegate, you can literally work yourself to death. You can also limit what can be accomplished.

Delegation is that characteristic which causes people to know they are part of the team because they have been given something to do and trusted to complete the task.

Delegation is a key to a successful leader. It is very difficult to achieve goals by ourselves.

> Major General Perry Smith, Air Force, Retired, says, "The best leaders understand that leadership is a liberation of talent; hence, they gain power, not only by consistently giving it away, but also not grabbing it back."

Years ago, I was a jet instructor pilot. There were some key words I remember of that experience. The instructor pilot would demonstrate how to do a particular maneuver. The instructor would then talk the student through the same maneuver. The third step was to let the student do it themselves. The words of transition were very specific, "You've got the stick." To which the student replied," I've got the stick." When the student says "I've got the stick" it meant "I," as the instructor, needed to take my hand off the stick. In the corporate world when we delegate to someone, we are basically saying the same thing. We're giving a person the control and we're taking our hand off of it and saying you have the authority to accomplish this particular task.

Great leaders surround themselves with people who are greater than themselves and who they can trust and then empower with specific tasks. President Ronald Reagan said to surround yourself with people who you can delegate to and not interfere with their job.

How do we apply delegation? It's very simple—we give it away. When we give our authority away to do a particular task the impact on the organization is monumental. Those people who have a new task to do will know that you have confidence in them. You can use their abilities to bring the organization to new heights.

A hurdle to overcome in delegation is not having confidence or trust in anyone else to do the job. Self-centeredness on the part of the leader can be the Achilles heel of a leader. Releasing control can be overcome by having the right team around you to do the job and then letting them do it. The key is in developing the right team that has the capabilities to accomplish the mission at hand.

VISION

Sight for the Future

Anticipating what might come

L eaders are visionaries. They process a steady influx of information, and then formulate a plan to make a possibility become true reality.

When entering the national command center in the Pentagon, where serious issues are handled, there is this quote on a wall taken from the Old Testament, which states, "Where there is no vision, the people perish." Vision is the characteristic of the leader to have foresight, to be able to look ahead, to envision what might happen in the future. Vision is something a leader not only possesses, but if they're wise, will seek input from the leadership team and others before concluding the right direction to go in the years ahead.

Many things should be considered as the vision materializes, but once the vision is complete and written down it needs to be communicated to the organization. Having a vision is essential for the team, business, fighter squadron, or church. Without it, "the people will perish."

Author Helen Keller, when asked what would be worse than being born blind, responded, "To have sight without vision."

Herb Kellerher, CEO of Southwest Airlines, says his vision is to have a company where "kindness and the human spirit are nurtured," where you "do what customers want and are happy in your work."

Abraham Lincoln said, "Vision is a clear, concise statement of the direction your organization should be going and justifies the actions you take."

Jack Welch, former chairman and CEO of General Electric, wrote that the effective leader leads through vision.

Vision is inspiration that motivates. Vision gives us a sense of purpose, work, and sacrifice. We can all buy into future plans so we are working together for a common goal.

There are *three* subheadings in this characteristic called vision. Once the vision is cast and articulated nothing will occur unless three things happen:

1. *Planning.* We should plan if we are to successfully fulfill a vision. Planning needs to be very meticulous. All factors must be considered. We need to plan in such a way that no stone is left unturned. We carefully plan and then we execute with "rigid flexibility." Planning is essential in order to see a vision accomplished

2. *Goal Setting.* In the process of planning we set goals, both short term and long term. Short term goals are easily measurable, so we can determine if things are going too fast or too slow. Goal setting causes the team to stretch itself, to reach forward, to accomplish what they did not think they could accomplish. Goals should not be set so high the organization knows they can never attain them. A reasonable goal causes people to stretch and do more than they ever thought possible.

3. *Initiative.* There are many good visions with good planning and good goal setting that never come to fruition because the leader does not have the courage to take the initiative.

When vision, planning, goal setting, and initiative all come together in a reasonable way and are accurately communicated, then you'll see some action. Some would say that casting a vision isn't necessary today. I would suggest vision is more important today than ever. Our nation will stagnate and perish without a vision.

President Abe Lincoln said, "We must plan for the future, because those who insist on living in the present are married to the past."

John Maxwell in his book Developing the Leader Within You

wrote, "With vision the leader is on a mission and a contagious spirit is felt among the crowd until others begin to rise alongside the leader."

Yes, vision can and will happen. The question is, could you be a leader who will look ahead and see the great things waiting to be accomplished?

JUSTICE

Are the Scales Balanced?

To do what is right and just

When you enter the Supreme Court building in Washington, D.C., there is a statue of a person dressed in a long robe with an arm held high grasping a scale. The scale is balanced. One side is not higher than the other. It is a reflection of how justice should be implemented.

The characteristic of justice in a leader is very important. This quality is equitableness. It is doing what is right, not in the eyes of the media or the public, but doing the right thing, the right way, for the right reason. It is the forming of an opinion and coming to a conclusion after all of the circumstances have been considered.

Justice is an essential characteristic, because in the course of leadership and working with people, there will be times when justice needs to be exercised.

Justice brings us to the position of righteousness or moral principle of determining just conduct. Regardless of whether it is the janitor or the CEO, everyone is special, important and deserves to be treated in a just way. We all need to be accountable. We can look at recent failures of corporate leaders who failed and landed in jail because they took from the lowly and stockholders to "feather their own nests." This same trait of justice is true in raising children; there shouldn't be any favorites. All should be raised and loved equally.

Just as plants in a garden have different needs for healthy growth, so do our children and team/work mates. As we study their personalities, talents, weaknesses, and strengths we can determine how to provide proper leadership. This applies individually as well as corporately.

Commitment to impart justice to all men, regardless of status, is equally important. This ability reflects integrity and courage and requires much wisdom.

Justice is not considered to be important by many because they may not have been treated justly themselves. As you read this chapter, think about your own life and if justice has always been exercised on your behalf, and how you felt when it wasn't. You, as a leader, now have the responsibility of making a judgment, weighing the facts and balancing the scale. The same would be true of how you would want to be treated. Yes, it would be good if we got all the breaks and somebody else got the drakes. But that isn't fair or just. Think of justice as one of the prime characteristics you want to exercise in your leadership, striving to treat others as you would have them treat you. Regardless of our rank or position, all who we lead deserve to be treated justly, respected, and made to feel important and special.

EXAMPLE

Just Like the Monkeys

A pattern or model

Being an example is being a model for others to follow. It is living a life another would want to copy. You never know who is watching you. This thought was captured in the following poem that was shared with me when our son, Tim, was five years old.

> A father and son were walking along the beach one day. The boy was lagging behind and suddenly gave a joyous shout of satisfaction: "Look, Daddy. I'm walking in your footsteps!" This simple statement made the man realize that he had to set a reasonable pace. It also spoke to his heart about giving spiritual leadership to his youngster.

> An unknown author has written:
> A careful man I ought to be;
> A little fellow follows me.
> I do not dare to go astray,
> For fear he'll go the selfsame way.
> Not once can I escape his eyes;
> What ere he sees me do he tries.
> Like me he says he's going to be,
> That little chap who follows me.
> I must remember as I go
> Through summer sun and winter snow,
> I'm molding for the years to be ...
> That little chap who follows me.

The standard is a life of integrity. In everything, set an example in all you do or say is a 24/7 challenge. Think of your life and the impact you make, starting in your home. When married, the husband should be an example to his wife and children. The greatest example a parent can provide to his children is to love their mother. The greatest impact a mate can have on their family comes from a life that is an example of love, tenderness, consideration, and giving of themselves

110%. Serving and putting others first is one of the best characteristics one can possess and pass on in the marketplace and especially at home.

Most people have been to a zoo. When they go, they usually take a few moments to visit the monkey cage. It is not unusual for visitors (maybe you are one of them) to make faces or do silly things and watch to see if the monkeys imitate you. Personally, I find it interesting to sit back and watch the people and not the monkeys. Transfer this mimicking to life. Remember, you are on display and being watched in your home, your workplace, at the service station, the theatre, driving your car, or in the grocery store. How you act and/or react will be observed by people. Good, bad, or indifferent, they will think if their leader acts a certain way they can, too.

There are three subheadings in this characteristic of being an example. A good example in your attitude can cause others to react or respond in a similar manner. The metaphorically half-full glass is used many times. An optimist calls it half full; a pessimist calls it half empty. What would we call it if there were one drop of water in it? Our attitude should be positive because at least we have one drop of water; now what will we do with that drop?

Example 1: *Attitude.* "Babe" Zaharias, a great track athlete, Olympian, and champion golfer, was playing in a tournament and hit the ball in the rough. When she found it she hit it on the green and sank the putt. When she removed the ball from the hole she realized it wasn't hers. That infraction resulted in a two stroke penalty. After the match was over (which she lost by one stroke) one of her friends said, "Babe, why did you say anything, nobody would have known?" Babe's response, I am told, was, "I would have known, and it would have stayed with me the rest of my life." You see in Babe the attitude of integrity and courage. Her example has had an ongoing influence.

Ben Franklin said, "Example is the school of mankind; they will learn at no other."

Coach Bill McCartney said, "Your attitude is four times as important as your actual physical abilities."

Example 2: *Enthusiasm*. If you want your people to be enthusiastic, you have to be enthusiastic. It is the passionate exuberance that is contagious to all. Regardless of the situation, think of that one drop of water and be enthusiastic that you have a drop of water. You see that blade of grass in the desert? If that drop fell on him, he would be rejoicing and saying, "Wow, I got a drink today!" Some remember Knute Rockne, the former Notre Dame football coach who was known for his locker room speeches to fire up the Fighting Irish. If Rockne's head was down and he had said, "Oh, woe is me!" the Irish would have reflected the same. Enthusiasm in your gait, in your speech, in your carriage. It is setting a model to those you're leading.

Example 3: *Endurance*. There are those who believe as they get more senior in rank or position that they don't need to work as hard. If you talk to most leaders they'll tell you as you climb the ladder of success there are more and more demands on your time. Leaders have to work harder and longer and put more energy into their position. Today in this electronic age, endurance is even more critical because we are tethered to our jobs by cell phones, Blackberrys, and pagers. Leaders must have endurance for the 24/7 environment we live in, not comparing how it was in the "good old days." Endurance is the perseverance to hang in there when tough times get tougher.

In the '84 Olympics, an athlete was running a marathon. He came in last due to an injury he sustained during the event. All had completed the race. It was dark and lights had to be turned on in the stadium. He crossed the finish line to a standing ovation. When asked why he didn't quit he responded, "My country didn't send me to just enter the race, but to finish it."

What's your example? Are you being that special person who is providing inspired influence on the home front as well as at work? Only you can answer that question. The application is clear. Example is 24/7 in attitude, enthusiasm, and endurance. Who's looking at you?

We have hurdles to overcome because it involves disciplining ourselves. We may have never grabbed on to the thought that "I can be an example and mentor to others," but in fact, we are all influencing "someone" and have the potential to be involved in influencing the lives of those we lead.

- A good leader's attitude should be to think like a winner.

- A winner is always ready to tackle something new.

- A winner isn't afraid of competition.

- A winner knows sometimes he's wrong and willing to admit it.

- A winner recognizes a problem as a challenge.

- A winner realizes there is no time like the present to get the job done.

- A winner thinks positively, acts positively, and lives positively.

- "Be A Winner"

COMMUNICATION

What's That, You Say?

Exchanging information

It is difficult to say which of the characteristics of a leader is more important. They all dovetail together. Certainly integrity is the launch pad because it ranks as one of the most important characteristics of a leader whether at home, in the office, the community, the church, on the team, or in the school house.

Where then does communication place in the characteristics for a leader? How would you define it? There are definitions from Webster's dictionary, but simply stated it is an imparting or exchanging of thoughts, opinions, and information. It is the interchange of sending messages back and forth. In the information age in which we live communication is more important than ever. There are two basics that are absolutely essential to understand:

1. God gave us two ears and one mouth. We need to listen twice as much as we speak. Many are challenged by the need to listen. Listening is the best preparation for speaking. We learn from listening not from talking.

2. The message received is always the one that counts. Let me explain. If I write a letter, send an email or text message, or have another form of communication and know what I want to get across, but the receiver does not receive it in the same light, then the communication is not complete. There are many reasons for this: it may be the impact of the demands on the other person, it could be issues at home or other things that would distract the receiver. The fact of the matter is it is the message received that counts. And the person responsible for insuring the receiver understands is always the sender. A good principle to follow is to know that the meaning of a message is in the mind of the receiver.

A manager was interviewing a technical expert about his services and fees. He asked the expert, "How much do you charge?"

The expert answered, "I charge $700 to answer three of your questions."

The manager then asked, "Isn't that awfully high?"

The expert replied, "Not really. Now what's your third question?"

Okay, that's an exaggeration of what you'll face with some experts. Like many jokes, it holds some insight. When you're talking to specialists, remember: Information is their product, and they want to be paid for all of it. Before you ask for specific information, ask if there's any charge for it. It's a good way to make sure the joke is not on you.

So how do we apply communication to our lives as leaders? There are certain basics of which to be aware. If, in fact, the message received is the one that counts; the sender must ensure the message is received in the same light it was sent. To do so there should be a clarifying of what was said or sent. Many times the message needs to be restated, sometimes even summarized. As was said in the first point, the art of listening is extremely important in communication. It is more important to listen than to speak.

Listening is the key to understanding. Listening is an art, a skill, even a discipline. Listening needs to be an active trait of the communication characteristic of a leader. There are some do's and don'ts of communication. Here are five "To Do's" that should help:

1. Create an environment where a person feels at ease and can talk openly.

2. Show interest in what the other person is saying.

3. Be patient.

4. Listen attentively.

5. Control your emotions and watch your body language.

Five things not to do when communicating:

1. Don't be working on other projects, tasks, or appear distracted.

2. Don't condescend.

3. Don't interrupt.

4. Don't say "you never" or "you always."

5. Don't jump to conclusions.

Major General Perry Smith, U.S. Air Force, retired, has said this, "The most important skill in leaders is listening. Squinting with your ears."

God's Word says that even a fool is wise when he keeps silent.

Pastor Tommy Nelson's wife has told him to "listen with his face." In other words, communicate with your eyes as well as with words. Body language says a lot.

Communication is something we need to provide on a regular basis. The impact on the organization is tremendous. Think about how life would be if we had no communication. We can readily see that as a leader we fail miserably without good communication skills.

The hurdles to overcome are best reflected when we look in the mirror, because communication is clearly a personal thing that effective leaders need to display and develop every day.

In today's electronic age, which could also be called the impersonal era, we avoid looking in each other's eyes, listening to the tone of another's voice, and "reading" body languages. Emailing and text messaging disallows personal contact. I can email my daughter, ask her how she is, and she can reply that she's "just fine." If I hear her voice when she responds, I can tell if she really is "just fine" or if something is bothering her. The impact of impersonalization can be disastrous.

I recall when our third daughter was in her first job after becoming an R.N. She worked in at a pediatric intensive care unit at Children's Hospital in Washington, D.C. When she would call and say, "Dad," I could tell by the tone of her voice that one of her young patients had died. She often could not speak after the initial greeting, but needed to hear words of tender encouragement.

SENSITIVITY

The Beat of the Heart

Responsiveness to feelings of others

Sensitivity can best be defined as being aligned and understanding the feelings and emotions of others. Today, more than any time, we have a society that has a beckoning call for leaders who have a sensitive spirit. This came home to me when I was on the USS Theodore Roosevelt as she was beginning a deployment to Bosnia. As I moved around the various areas of that great aircraft carrier and spoke to the young sailors, I asked what they desired most in a leader. Their response could be summed up in one word: authenticity.

What is authenticity? It is being "real." Young people (and seniors, too) don't want their leaders to be hypocrites. They want leaders who understand their own personal frailties, and understand the emotions and feelings of those who are working for them as well.

Most of us have seen leaders we'd like to emulate. Some saw the film Patton and wanted to be a leader like Patton, others wanted to be a leader like Tom Landry, former coach of the Dallas Cowboys, or maybe a Jack Welch at General Electric. All three were individuals who showed sensitivity to the spirits of those they were leading. They impacted people personally, not just in ways that counted in the win-loss column or in the bottom line.

LaDonna Witmer, a poet who was speaking at a conference at Willow Creek Community Church in Barrington, Illinois, gave some hard points of what her generation (i.e. the X Generation) wanted from their leaders, parents, and teachers. She explained who "X-ers" were, saying:

1. We are homesick for a place we've never heard.

2. Jaded and cynical; we've seen it all.

3. We come from broken homes where promises were not kept.

4. Truth is what we call it.

5. We are better at seeking than finding.

Her closing comment at this conference was, "Don't give up on us; we're searching." She was giving an example of the ills of our country.

We're in trouble when broken homes contribute to three out of every four suicides. We're in trouble when educational reform substitutes for parental relationships. LaDonna Witmer said in the end the most important thing is this: be authentic. When so many young people come from a latch-key home, a broken home, a fatherless society, we as leaders need to be authentically sensitive to those we lead. People may not want to admit it, but most will respond better to a leader who has a sensitive spirit.

When I was a lieutenant and an aide to a general, he said to get as close to your people as you can, but not so close that you can't discipline them. As I have reflected on that comment, I'm challenged to be sensitive to people and really get close to them so our hearts are beating together. One of several young men who were influenced in our home became a Navy commander. Andy would daily make rounds of his ship, the USS Fife, and converse with his sailors. If they seemed to want to talk, Andy would invite them to his quarters in the evening and spend one on one time, sharing and talking. Andy was loved by those under his command.

I recall seeing a video clip that could be a "discussion starter" for your teenagers. It presented a party where drugs and alcohol were present. When first looking at it on the screen, the picture was all out of focus until one of the girls at this party reached up and took off her clear plastic mask. Then she was in focus. The young girl justified wearing the mask by stating this was the only way she could have friends. The mask she wore covered her true identity.

Today, people—young and old—wear masks. All of us have a tendency to wear them. It is only when we become vulnerable (and take off our mask) that we'll be effective and authentic leaders. Our hearts beating together is a sign we are sensitive to one another.

The hurdles we face are our inabilities to take off our own masks, to get vulnerable with people and see behind their masks.

In my last five leadership positions spanning over twenty years, I would tell my team what was expected of them and encourage them to take off their masks so I could help them succeed. I let them know they were trusted and could trust me. I became available to discuss any problems, personal or professional. I found my open-door policy was an encouragement to many.

HUMAN RESPONSIBILITY

My Brother's Keeper

Taking care of the needs of people

This characteristic of a leader is to understand that he is responsible for his people. Human responsibility is different from human rights. Some believe human rights allow them to demand what they think they deserve. Human responsibility is leaders understanding they are responsible for the men and women who work for them. It is care taking and realizing the need for job satisfaction. It is taking care of the needs of your people—in many aspects other than in the office. It is the capacity to recognize moral decisions and the needs and challenges people have in the normal course of living.

Years ago there was failed leadership in the Philippines and the president had to leave. I've often thought about President Marcos. If he had only understood human responsibility and the need for the care and feeding of the people of the Philippines he would have ensured their well-being. He would not have left the presidency in disgrace, but with a legacy of which all Philippine people could have been proud.

The Good Book says right in the beginning, "Am I my brother's keeper?"

The answer is yes. If you are the leader, you are your brother's keeper.

So often of late we have seen examples of CEOs, chairmen of corporations, and CFOs who have abused their power. They've taken care of themselves and possibly their senior leadership, but they have taken from and harmed people, leaving spirits completely broken. These leaders have unjustly taken from workers and not ensured their safety, security, and well-being. What a sad commentary on this type of self-serving leadership.

Human responsibility, when applied appropriately, can cause people to want to "take the hill" and wholeheartedly follow the person who is leading. There are stories about slaves whose masters understood human responsibility. When freed, those slaves did not want to leave their leader/master.

The future of mankind is waiting for those who will come to understand their role and take up the responsibilities for all living things. It is our responsibility to take care of and provide for our people. We all want to be successful. Success is personal. If, however, you want to have a life of significance, you work to ensure the success of your people.

> President John F. Kennedy said, "Ask not what your country can do for you, but ask what you can do for your country."

As a leader we should then say "not what these people can do for me, but what can I do for my people." When that occurs (which is out of step with society today), you will find people who have a job satisfaction rating off the charts. It will be a place where people will want to work because they know the leadership looks after them.

One of the best examples today would be Chick-fil-A. Their founder and chairman Truett Cathy looks after his people. You can look quickly at a corporation, an organization, a military unit, see how many people love coming to work and if their turnover of employees is low. These are indications of job satisfaction that result from positive leadership. You'll see an organization where the leader is someone who understands human responsibility and not only understands, but ensures his people's needs are met.

CONFIDENCE

Credible

Assurance, full trust

Confidence is one of those things that can be an asset and yet at the same time, if misapplied, can be a great detriment to a leader. When one believes they are above the law, above the rules, above their people, confidence turns into cocky arrogance. These people become self-centered and obnoxious to the people who work with them. A person who is confident knows what he needs to do, how he should do it, and knows the people he has placed around him. He is able to exude a spirit of trust and credibility that will carry his leadership and his team a long way.

Certainly, integrity fits into confidence because a leader of integrity is well-grounded and confident that they are doing the right thing for the right reasons. The Book says "pride comes before destruction and a haughty spirit before a fall." Humble confidence is the opposite of cocky arrogance.

Earlier we talked about the comparison of pride and brokenness. It's a great example of how one can believe in himself and be haughty or have that spirit of a servant leader.

Proud, Unbroken People	Broken People
Have to prove that they are right	Are willing to yield the right to be right
Claim rights	Yield rights
Have a demanding spirit	Have a giving spirit
Are self-protective of time, rights, reputation	Are self-denying
Desire to be served	Are motivated to serve others

I'd like to relate confidence and cockiness to an athlete. One athlete reads his clippings and puts them aside and presses on. The other one reads all of the clippings and adulation and believes them. We need to believe in ourselves, be confident, not cocky, and have trust in other people.

A close friend of mine, Ben Manthei, has said, "Are you looking for success or significance?" Success is self-focused; significance is focused on those who are working with us. Ben has it right.

The application of confidence comes in how we approach our daily activities and our interaction with people. Do they see someone who is confident and looks them in the eye and who can communicate well? Do they have the loyalty of the individual? Do they build respect in their confidence? Respect is something that is earned; it does not come with a title, or position, or parking place. If one relies on their title for respect, it's as thin as the ink on the page. When promoted to general, I had positional respect. Earned respect is accomplished through servant leadership and by having integrity on and off the job.

Confidence is something each leader needs to apply on a daily basis. As interaction with his people takes place, confidence in him will grow. It will be based on confidence and not cockiness.

> In an attempt to get the focus off himself, a leader and friend of mine said, "Don't look at me because I'll fail you. Look at the One Who has never failed." And that's the God who created us.

The impact of our personal confidence on our organization and in our home life is monumental. The people we work with, our families, those in our community, will look to someone who has confidence, who is self-assured, not prideful, boastful, or arrogant, but who has a humble servant's heart.

When we look at hurdles to overcome, a cocky attitude is first on the list. Confidence is personal. We need to guard ourselves against being prideful or arrogant and be on guard for those attributes that are a hindrance to healthy confidence. A good lesson in how not to be over confident is to put your fist into a bucket of water, then take it out and look for an impression left in the water. This tells us we may not be as important in other's eyes as we are in our own.

TEAMWORK

You Can't Do It Alone

Performing together in harmony

It is natural for a coach to talk about teamwork. Fisher DeBerry, the former coach at the Air Force Academy, said, "We win together!"

In the course of my life I've provided leadership in a number of different venues. I'm absolutely convinced that teamwork is essential. Teamwork can be defined as a group of people, large or small, pulling in the same direction to accomplish one or more tasks in a way that can be beneficial to them and the organization they represent.

Teamwork is also important in the home. In the original version of the movie Cheaper By the Dozen, the dad is a stern disciplinarian who delegates to the children and keeps the team functioning. In the newer version of this film, the kids have various responsibilities, but they fail to accomplish tasks as a team. The lack of leadership and teamwork keep the home from functioning well, and although funny to watch, it would be a sad reality in real life.

One of our daughters has eight children. Their house runs pretty well because there is a list of responsibilities for every one. The tasks are changed so the children do not get bored in fulfilling their responsibilities to the team. We can all learn from that approach.

Teamwork also applies to a husband and wife. Somebody said in a counseling session that teamwork and marriage is a 50/50 proposition. But in real life if you are going to have a successful marriage, it is not 50/50, it's 100/100, giving of ourselves completely to meeting the needs of one another. Each one giving completely of themselves to one other for the greater good is a key to a strong team, in the home or workplace.

Getting back to the sports world, the business world, or the military, we come to teamwork which is essential. It has been said, "A team is only as strong as its weakest link." I would certainly agree, but I also know a leader's responsibility is to take the "weakest link" and help that person become an all-star through training, encouragement, resources, or anything that will bring them to the level of the others on the team. It is the leader who has to make those "how to" decisions.

Often when we look at teamwork we realize there are people on the team who are playing "out of position." We have them in jobs they are not gifted in or don't like and they balk at them or fail and become discouraged and even quit. But if they are placed in another position where they are challenged and have a desire to perform, we as leaders will benefit from it because they will use their gifts and skills that will enhance the whole team. They will have personal fulfillment. Occasionally if all our efforts fail, the "weak link" may move on to a different venue, hopefully better prepared for success because of our leadership in their life.

> The Good Book has a verse on teamwork in Ecclesiastes 4:9–12. It says, "one may be overpowered, two can defend themselves; a cord of three strands cannot be easily broken."

If you can, picture someone with a cord with one strand and how easy it would be to take two fingers to pull it apart. But take two strands, bind them together, and then try to pull them apart. It becomes very difficult to break. Three strands would be even harder. That's a good picture of teamwork. We are bound together for a common purpose to be successful in our accomplishments.

The application of teamwork from a leadership standpoint is to be able to assure our entire team is working together, using their gifts and talents in their positions, and we are looking after each other. If one is weak, the leader and others will seek to help that person become an all-star for the team.

At the Marine Corps recruit training base at Parris Island a recruit, a pretty fast lad, came running in after finishing an event saying, "I won! I won! I won!" The drill sergeant said, "What did you win?" He said, "I won, finished ahead of everyone else!" And the drill sergeant said, "What did you win? I don't see your squad with you. Go back, get with your squad, and bring them with you."

There's a great lesson in application. Leaders must not out-distance the team. If we are going to be a team; we need to work together. This is so true in organizations and homes regardless of the size or numbers. Teamwork is important in the military, corporations, universities, marching bands, sports, and in every home. Teamwork is a force multiplier and helps us do even greater things because of the strength in numbers pulling together.

Some of the challenges in teamwork would be to recognize people as individuals, encouraging and applying teamwork. Training people to be strong team members who look after one another and empower the team to do their very best is the goal of the leader. Remember that a team is a group of individuals having differing needs while pursuing a common goal.

TRAINING

Practice, Practice, Practice

Practice, practice, practice

The key to effective teamwork is practice, practice, practice. Training is the development and forming of habits and behavior to make us proficient by repetition. It is the giving of instruction, and discipline that goes along with training. Training allows us to know what to do but it provides mental toughness. We always know what we're to do. A human resources manager said, "The best trainer is the behavior of the leader." Example, discipline, and many other characteristics accumulate in training.

Many leaders make the mistake of thinking when a new person joins their team with a resume replete with their experience, that the "new guy" doesn't need to be trained. Every team/organization has its own personality. There is a uniqueness, and culture, in each organization that is a reflection of its leadership. Thus the "new boy on the block" still needs training.

My first employment after I retired from the Air Force was on the senior staff of the US Olympic Committee. I was so impressed with the discipline and training that athletes of all sports put into practice. They trained to a level that I had not experienced in all of my life, even though I had been involved in the athletic community for many years. All of the athletes aspired to win the gold medal. The US Olympic Committee, through its sports medicine and sports science, worked with each athlete to develop them to their maximum potential. I learned quickly that the difference between a gold medal and no medal might be a 100th of a second. The athletes training in many cases started well before the sun came up, and with some lasted until dark. They provided me with a good example of how one truly trains and reminded me of how Coach Paul Brown, who formed the Cleveland Browns years ago, developed the athletes in their training camp. He had gold medal Olympic champion sprinter Jessie Owens train the players how to run. Then they practiced, and practiced, and practiced some more.

Remember, practice, practice, practice. Train and do not get so busy with normal activities that you don't spend time training.

Training is ongoing. There is a continuing need for training. Look to new techniques, seminars, and anything that keeps the dynamics of your expertise exciting. Good trainers are those who have the trainee involved.

Proverbs 22:6 says to "train a child in the way he should go and when he is old he will not depart from it." This is a good example of successful training.

Mark Twain said training is everything. The question is: are we allowing people time to be trained? Are we being trained ourselves to increase our personal skills? Today there are many available courses, seminars, lectures, and conferences in all subjects. Add to that the internet and all the information available there and we realize we have a continuum for any discipline or subject.

When we look at the application of training, we realize we need to look at each individual within our organization to see the gifts and talents they bring to the table. Then we must learn how we can maximize these strengths through additional training.

The impact on the organization is greater professionalism, high quality, and standards. As each team member improves, so does the organization.

A hurdle to overcome is the possibility of becoming so busy with daily activities that we don't allow time for training. Another hurdle is that we are not sensitive to instruction. Prideful attitudes ("I don't need that") will curtail the training process and progress.

If a leader is sensitive to the need for training, he will be sensitive to those opportunities and ensure his team avails themselves for the betterment of the entire organization. That's how you build up a team.

RELAXATION

Hanging Loose

To bring relief from stress

Relaxing is one of the biggest challenges leaders have today. The most effective leaders are those who are able to relax, get away, to be with family and friends, to literally "chill out" so they can come back to the job refreshed and ready to take on the challenges of the day. "Chilling out" applies to family and friends, as well as with teammates.

Companies and the military give leave time, but many times the leader feels like he is indispensable and cannot be away. This is a big error because all of us need to relax. A burned-out leader cannot effectively lead.

In today's world it's even more difficult. Relaxing used to be leaving the office for home to be with your wife and children, or if single, to go out with friends. Today, that's almost impossible to do. With the electronic age, we are all "tethered." Just think of the cell phone, text messaging, iPods, and Blackberrys. All those electronics tether us to the job. Even in the "old days" we had a type of primitive cell phone we called "the brick" that kept us tied to our job.

Another challenge today is being tied to the computer at home. One used to go home, to the quietness of their own place, and relax, read a book, watch television, visit with friends, and be with their spouse and children. Now many a leader will go home, have dinner, and then get on the computer until late in the evening. We cannot seem to take our hands and eyes off of it. We believe that's the only way to be successful, when in fact, if we relax and get away and turn our minds off work, we will come back refreshed and much more effective.

Recently we went on a cruise with our children. The five couples on the journey were actively involved in the workplace. All were tied electronically to the "work station." When the ship was about ten minutes away from the dock, our cell phones became inoperative, and unless you went to the business center you were completely out of touch. I must say, the wives were very happy because they knew that for the period of the cruise they would have the complete attention of their mate. Each of us was able to relax in a way we would not have been able to had we been electronically bound.

Cut the "tether." You'll never regret it. The characteristic of discipline is what is needed. We have to discipline ourselves to relax, and indeed we have to have the courage to relax. By your example your teammates will follow you. Start today.

Unwind. Life is tiring. Our minds and our hearts are weary. Often the best thing we can do is to relax. There is a saying that laughter is the best medicine. Abraham Lincoln said "Don't forget that humor is a major component in your ability to persuade people. A good laugh is good for both mental and physical digestion."

> In Psalm 46:10, it is written, "Be still, and know that I am God." Stillness, a quietness of spirit, a quietness of mind. Just being able to quietly relax.

Relaxing on the job is also important. We get so caught up in daily activities, we don't have time to do any constructive thinking. It seems we are always in react mode, when in fact we need to take time to think, relax, and get away from the daily grind.

The impact on the organization is monumental because a leader who knows how to relax is one who is most effective. He also is a leader who ensures his people have time to relax. A good leader, sensitive to his teammates, encourages time away from work, monitors "workaholics," and plans for times of corporate relaxation. A team that plays together usually stays together.

Probably the greatest hurdle to overcome is living in a society that is so fast paced that we don't take time out to just "cool it."

A former CEO of Coca Cola spoke of the relationship of work to one's other commitments:

> Imagine life as a game in which you are juggling some five balls in the air. You name them—work, family, health, friends and spirit—and you're keeping all of these in the air. You will

soon understand that work is a rubber ball. If you drop it, it will bounce back. But the other four balls—family, health, friends, and spirit—are made of glass.

How?

If you drop one of these, they will be irrevocably scuffed, marked, nicked, damaged, or even shattered. They will never be the same. You must understand that and strive for balance in your life.

- Don't undermine your worth by comparing yourself with others. It is because we are different that each of us is special. Don't set your goals by what other people deem important. Only you know what is best for yourself.

- Don't take for granted the things closest to your heart. Cling to them as you would your life for without them, life is meaningless.

- Don't let your life slip through your fingers by living in the past or for the future. By living your life one day at a time you really live all the days of your life.

- Don't give up when you still have something to give. Nothing is really over until the moment you stop trying.

- Don't be afraid to admit that you are less than perfect. It is this fragile thread that binds us to each other.

- Don't be afraid to encounter risks. It is by taking chances that we learn how to be brave.

- Don't shut love out of your life by saying it's impossible to find. The quickest way to receive love is to give; the fastest way to lose love is to hold it too tightly; and the best way to keep love is to give it wings.

- Don't run through life so fast that you forget not only where you've been, but also where you are going.

- Don't forget a person's greatest emotional need is to feel appreciated.

- Don't hesitate to learn. Knowledge is invaluable. Don't use words carelessly. They cannot be retrieved.

- Life is not a race, but a journey to be savored each step of the way. Yesterday is History, Tomorrow is a Mystery, and Today is a Gift: that's why we call it the Present.

LOVE

The Greatest Four-Letter Word

Benevolent affection

L ove. The reason for love may be thought of as Valentine's Day or Christmas. Love is something that should run through our veins every day. I'm convinced one can be a good leader, even a great leader, but no one will maximize their ability as a leader unless they love their people.

What is love? It's defined in many ways. The concern for the well-being of others, selflessness, benevolent affection. It is truly caring for all aspects of those who work for you. It is loving in a way they understand how much you care for them. Loving people where they are, unconditionally.

> 1 Corinthians 13 states it well, "Faith, hope, and love; but the greatest of these is love." And "love never fails."

If love never fails, I'm challenged, and I hope you are, to really love your people. They need to see love in your actions and in your words. This is certainly true in the home. If you are married and have a mate and children they need to know you love them. Love them unconditionally in spite of themselves, not the way you would like them to be, but just the way they are. Love begins at home. We all need to have the strength to love one another—to be free to give love as well as accept love.

Mother Teresa said, "It's not how much we do, but how much we love and put it into action."

Love is that special ingredient that separates leaders. Leaders who love their people are leaders who maximize all of these characteristics, thus maximizing the people who work for them.

We need to remember we love people, not things. We use things, not people. That's a provocative statement because sometimes we use people and do not love them. In my observation, people always know when that's happening and it ruins our credibility with them.

As we draw to the last of our characteristics of a leader, we need to understand how important it is to love. To put it into a few words (I encourage you to memorize this):

Leading is loving; loving is serving. You see, loving is not just saying words, but it is an action we take that will impact people. The example of love permeates a person's whole spirit and you will find your team will do more for you than you had ever thought possible because they will know you love them.

William Shakespeare said it accurately, "They do not love that do not show their love." Leadership characteristics begin with integrity and conclude with love.

We have run the full gamut of the person of a leader. Where do you "fit" in your leadership role according to these characteristics? You can personally evaluate yourself by taking the Leadership Quiz at the end of this book.

CONCLUSION

We have spoken of principles and characteristics essential for a leader to be involved in influencing those he or she leads. Leadership, truly, is all about people. If it weren't for people, leadership would be easy. If it weren't for people, being the pastor of a church would be easy. If it weren't for people, being a headmaster of a school would be easy. If it weren't for people, being a coach would be easy. But leaders need people and must recognize, even in this fast-paced electronic age, people are our most valuable asset. We need to remember we lead people, and manage resources.

We have gone through a phase in our society when the focus was on management, thinking we manage people. Putting it in other words, we "used" people. When that happens, be assured you will have people problems that can have impacting consequences.

We've spoken only about one person in this short book, the leader. These are principles and characteristics essential to being an effective leader. Leadership starts with the individual and it begins with character. Character binds us together. Character is a 24/7 lifestyle. It is something we need to address for all leaders, because if a leader is not a person of character he or she will leave in the wake destroyed lives and families.

As we reflect on the above, we can probably all think of examples of failed leadership, and it often goes back to character flaws of that particular individual.

We also need to understand that our attitude, our example, our outlook, determines the outcome of our efforts.

Leaders have tremendous burdens placed upon them. They look after the bottom line to ensure the mission is accomplished. They must be a visionary. They must be all of the things we have spoken about in this book. One of the problems today is we allow society to determine our character instead of leaning on a strong foundation for leadership. For me, it's God's Word. I assure you of the need to have a foundation for your character. You must know what that is and ensure it is built on a solid rock.

The measure of a leader is found in the faces of their people. You can walk through the halls of any corporation, through the halls of a school, and look at the faces of the people and see if they are being led in a way that will cause them to reach maximum performance.

The question is, as we put all of these characteristics together, how can we ensure we keep a sharp edge in our character? We need a check list (maybe this book will help) or someone or something to hold us accountable so we don't get caught up in letting the world set our standards.

Not as Frank Sinatra said, "I'll do it my way," or as Nike says, "Just do it." Knowing what is right and then doing it, keeping check on ourselves to ensure we don't allow society to mold our standards and character. Are we a person of conviction or are we a chameleon? We are one or the other. It's our decision.

The challenge for each of us is to be men and women of character and conviction, who seek to provide inspired influence to those we lead. From the home to the marketplace, that's our challenge.

We are challenged to be leaders of sound character with strong convictions. Those in our sphere of influence will have confidence and trust in the leader who has "The Buck Stops Here" on their desk.

"The unexamined life is not worth living."

-Socrates

LEADERSHIP QUIZ

The following instrument is provided for you to measure your growth as a leader. Read each of the characteristics and evaluate yourself using the following:

1–Don't understand

2–No, that's not me

3–That's me sometimes

4–That's me often

5–Yes, that's definitely me

1. Integrity

Uprightness of character and soundness of moral principle, absolute truthfulness, and honesty.

     1   2   3   4   5

2. Knowledge

Acquired information, including professional knowledge and understanding of your men and women.

     1   2   3   4   5

3. Decisiveness

Ability to reach decisions promptly without being autocratic and to announce them in a clear, positive manner.

     1   2   3   4   5

4. Courage

Mental quality that recognizes fear of danger or criticism but enables an individual to proceed in the face of it with calmness and firmness.

1   2   3   4   5

5. Dependability

The certainty of the proper performance of duty.

1   2   3   4   5

6. Discipline

To train or develop by instruction and exercise self-control. To bring under control.

1   2   3   4   5

7. Delegation

To have others represent you. The commission given to a person or group.

1   2   3   4   5

8. Vision

Ability to describe the future in present terms. Focus on goal setting, planning, and initiative.

1   2   3   4   5

9. Justice

The quality of being impartial and consistent in exercising command. Weighing of facts, possible solutions, and then using good judgment.

1   2   3   4   5

10. Example

The ability to practice what one preaches. Having a positive attitude. Being an enthusiastic leader. Presenting and living a lifestyle that encompasses tact and the other characteristics of a leader. Having the endurance to get the job done.

1   2   3   4   5

11. Communication

Creating open channels of communication both in speech and hearing.

1   2   3   4   5

12. Sensitivity

Showing empathy, consideration, recognition, and praise of your people. Avoiding focusing on self, but looking to serve others.

1   2   3   4   5

13. Human Responsibility

Focus on taking care of the needs of your people.

1   2   3   4   5

14. Confidence

Being secure in how God has gifted you. Not arrogant or cocky but a leader who has self-confidence without being egotistical.

1   2   3   4   5

15. Teamwork

Understand the importance of others in accomplishing tasks. Being loyal both down and up in the chain of command.

1   2   3   4   5

16. Training

Giving people the tools and skills they need to succeed.

1   2   3   4   5

17. Relaxation

Patient under pressure. Have a sense of humor—being able to laugh and have a happy face.

1   2   3   4   5

18. Love

Love the people that follow you and be sure they know you do.

1   2   3   4   5

APPENDIX

Selected Biblical References

Integrity

Proverbs 10:9, Proverbs 11:3, Proverbs 13:6, Titus 2:7, Daniel 6:3–5, Psalm 26; Job 31:5,6

Knowledge

Proverbs 1:7, Proverbs 8:10, Proverbs 8:14, Colossians 2:3

Decisiveness

Deuteronomy 30:19, Joshua 24:15, Proverbs 16:16

Courage

Joshua 1:6–9, 1 Corinthians 16:13, Philippians 1:28, 2 Chronicles 32:7, Hebrews 13:6

Dependability

Joshua 1:5, 1 Corinthians 16:13, Proverbs 18:24

Discipline

Proverbs 3:11, 1 Timothy 4:7, Titus 1:8

Delegation

Acts 1:7–8, Matthew 28:18

Vision

Psalm 119:18, Proverbs 29:18; Acts 26:19

Justice

John 5:30, Psalm 119:56, Proverbs 12:11, Proverbs 21:3, Proverbs 24:25, Philippians 4:5; Job 31:5,6; Luke 18:3

Example

1 Corinthians 11:1, 1 Timothy 4:12, Titus 2:7, Philippians 4:4–8; 1 Timothy 4:11–12

Communication

Psalm 19:3–4, Proverbs 22:11, 1 Timothy 4:11–13, 2 Corinthians 8:7

Sensitivity

Ephesians 4:2, Galatians 6:2, Proverbs 15:1

Human Responsibility

Genesis 4:9, Psalm 133:1, Galatians 5:11–15

Confidence

1 John 5:14, Philemon 1:25, Hebrews 4:16, Hebrews 10:19; Isaiah 32:17; Philippians 3:3

Teamwork

Ecclesiastes 4:9–12; Philippians 1:3–6

Training

Proverbs 22:6–7, 1 Corinthians 9:25, 2 Timothy 3:16

Relaxation

Proverbs 15:13–15, Matthew 11:28, Psalm 91:1, Exodus 31:15

Love

John 3:16, 1 Corinthians 13, Hebrews 10:24, 1 John 4:7–21, Romans 12:9–18

ABOUT THE AUTHOR

Dick Abel
Brigadier General, USAF (Retired)
Founder and President,
Leadership is all about People

Dick Abel founded *Leadership is all about People* and currently serves as president. *All about People* is a half-day seminar program that focuses on the person of the leader. Dick is an internationally known speaker on family values, military affairs, and moral leadership. When he presents the interactive seminar it focuses on four essential principles of leaders and eighteen characteristics that form our lives.

Dick retired as a Brigadier General in the United States Air Force. He was a pilot, led the War Hawk jet acrobatic team, and was an assistant football coach at the United States Air Force Academy. He is the father of four and grandfather of nineteen and has been a mentor to numerous young men.

During his thirty-year Air Force career he served three four-star Admirals and the Chairman of the Joint Chiefs of Staff. He also made five flights to escort returning POWs from Vietnam. His career concluded with his assignment as Director of Public Affairs, United States Air Force.

After retiring in 1985, Dick served on the senior staff of the U.S. Olympic Committee, later as National President of the Fellowship of Christian Athletes, and then became the Executive Director of the Military Ministry of Campus Crusade for Christ for fourteen years. That coupled with his thirty-year career makes Dick a forty-four-year servant to service members and their families who are focused on protecting the freedoms and way of life we enjoy in America.

He has served on many boards and has military decorations and awards from his time in the service. General Abel is married to the former Ann Voelcker from San Antonio and currently resides in the Hampton Roads area of Virginia.

MORE PRAISE FOR
THE DNA OF LEADERSHIP:

Corporate

"When we are in a position of leadership, we need all the help we can get. *The DNA of Leadership* offers an excellent checklist that not only helps hold us accountable at home and at work, but also helps us be successful at both."

Norm Miller
Chairman
Interstate Battery

"Too often, leadership becomes tainted and crippled by the brokenness of our own human nature. Our insecurities and self-centered interests diminish the positive effects of our positions of leadership. We fall into the trap of denial, blaming those we lead for lack of progress. This book is a cure for those ills as it sharply presents the fundamental principles of effective leadership and unleashes true power for those who humble themselves and put its wise instructions into practice."

Dan Arnold
Founder and President
Road Ranger Convenience Stores and Travel Centers

Media

"Dick Abel is a leader and knows the values each of us must embrace to become leaders. Abel's *The DNA of Leadership* guides us to self-knowledge and how to use that knowledge to lead."

David Hartman
Television Producer
Original Host, Good Morning America

Military

"Dick Abel has written an outstanding book on leadership. His unique approach makes reading it very worthwhile."

David C. Jones
General, USAF (Ret)
Chairman, JCS 1978–1982
Chief of Staff, USAF, USAF, 1974–1978

"This is a must read for people in positions of leadership and responsibility and those aspiring to success in life. Straightforward and compelling, Dick Abel's easy-to-understand guide outlines the essential principles and attributes of good leadership. It is all about people."

William "Fox" Fallon
Admiral US Navy (Ret)

"General Abel is *The DNA of Leadership*! He teaches it, he lives it, he believes it, he counsels folks on it and he constantly improves on it. I think it is evident by the way he has captured the foundational character principles and leaderships traits. I can think of no better person to teach anyone about leadership than General Abel simply because he is a man of character, conviction, believability and he has the experiences to back it up."

Gene Overstreet
Sergeant Major US Marine Corps [Ret]
President
Non-Commissioned Officers Association

"In *The DNA of Leadership* Dick Abel discusses one of the most overlooked yet most important qualities that any leader can possess: character. Few leaders will ever reach their full potential without exceptional character. Take a lesson from one of the U.S. Military, great leaders. Develop your character and develop your leadership influence through this book."

Jeff Struecker, author, speaker, soldier in Black Hawk Down
Major (Chaplain) U.S. Army

Ministry

"It has been my privilege to have known the general ever since he was stationed in Hawaii. I have watched him as he has grown in his Christian life and as a leader. He has exemplified the distinctive qualities as a leader in the Pacific Command, Hawaii, and serving the Chairman of the Joint Chiefs of Staff at the Pentagon. It is my distinct privilege to recommend this book to any and all who desire to lead in any context, in the home, the marketplace and the military."

Dr. James R. Cook
Founder and President
International Ministries, Inc.

"I have had the privilege of serving God with Dick Abel for many years. He is well qualified to teach about leadership, both from his rich experience and from the Bible."

Steve Douglass
President
Campus Crusade for Christ

Athletics

"This book on leadership covers the subject about as thoroughly as any I've read. *The DNA of Leadership* is a must read for those seeking how to be successful as a leader."

Bobby Bowden
Head Football Coach
Florida State University

"I am so glad that General Dick Abel has put a lot of his outstanding leadership qualities and ideas on paper. This is a must read for any person who aspires for a position of leadership."

Fisher DeBerry
Retired Air Force Academy Head Football Coach

"In recent years we've become convinced that DNA is an unquestionable test which reveals all truth in a given matter. Now, after a lifetime of leadership experience, serving his nation and major organizations, General Abel provides solid evidence on how to develop genuine leadership traits in this important book."

Les Steckel

President and CEO

Fellowship of Christian Athletes

Former NFL Player and Coach

Education

"Dick Abel is a confident, enthusiastic leader of exemplary character. In his book, *The DNA of Leadership*, Dick starts with integrity, the key to building trust and confidence, and charts a clear course to leadership success."

Jerry Allen

Major General, USAF (Ret)

Commandant

Virginia Tech Corps of Cadets

"Brigadier General Dick Abel has provided a very practical guide to life and effective leadership... it is also a blue print for being 'on-parade' 24/7 for young leaders."

General J.H.Binford Peay III

U.S.Army (Ret)

Superintendent

Virginia Military Institute

[former Commander U.S.Central Command]

"Your book is excellent and demonstrates that a publication doesn't have to be a certain length to have quality. I like the many leadership subjects addressed and brief but effective attention is given to them. I'd recommend the book both as a primer for those considering a leadership position or as a refresher for those already there but sometimes forget why. A job well done."

Gene Habecker

President

Taylor University

Politics

"Few individuals could be better qualified to write on leadership than Dick Abel. Rising to the rank of Brigadier General in the highly competitive field of Public Affairs in the USAF, he was not content to retire. He entered a new career of ministry and for fourteen years ministered to the spiritual needs of others. Now, as a grandfather, he continues to share his wide experience with others."

Vern Orr, PhD.
Secretary of the AF 1981–1985

"I know Dick Abel to be a leader. To make the rank of general tells you he is a leader. I personally watched him through my membership on the National Board of the Fellowship of Christian Athletes and my involvement with the Military Ministry; in fact he is a great leader. *The DNA of Leadership* will help many people in the future become the leaders they were meant to be."

Joe M. Rodgers
former US Ambassador to France
[1985–1989]